Mr. Shadow, My Friend

By Will McIntosh
Illustrated by Andrew Botting

An ethansLight Production

Parson's Porch Books

www.parsonsporchbooks.com

Mr. Shadow, My Friend
ISBN: Hardcover 9781946478818
Copyright © 2018 by Will McIntosh

All rights reserved. No part of this book may be reproduced or transmitted in any form or by any means, electronic or mechanical, including photocopying, recording, or by any information storage and retrieval system, without permission in writing from the publisher.

With much love and pride for my son, Ethan, who brings true joy and meaning to my life, and for the amazing teachers, therapists, volunteers, and medical professionals we have come to know who continue to bring a little bit of Heaven to us on this incredible journey.

— Will McIntosh

When the sun is shining bright for all the world to see,

I'm so happy to
see you today!

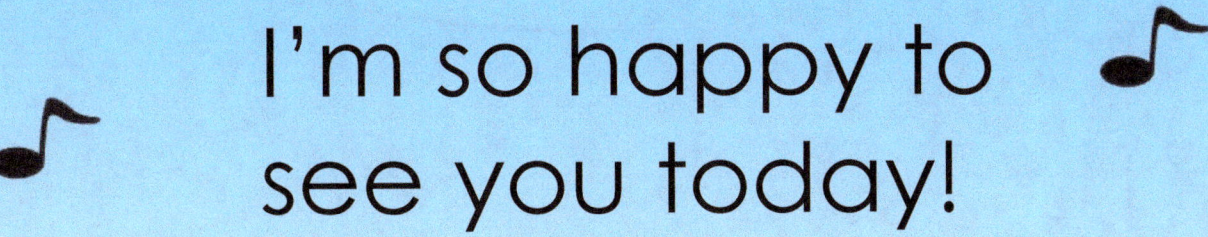

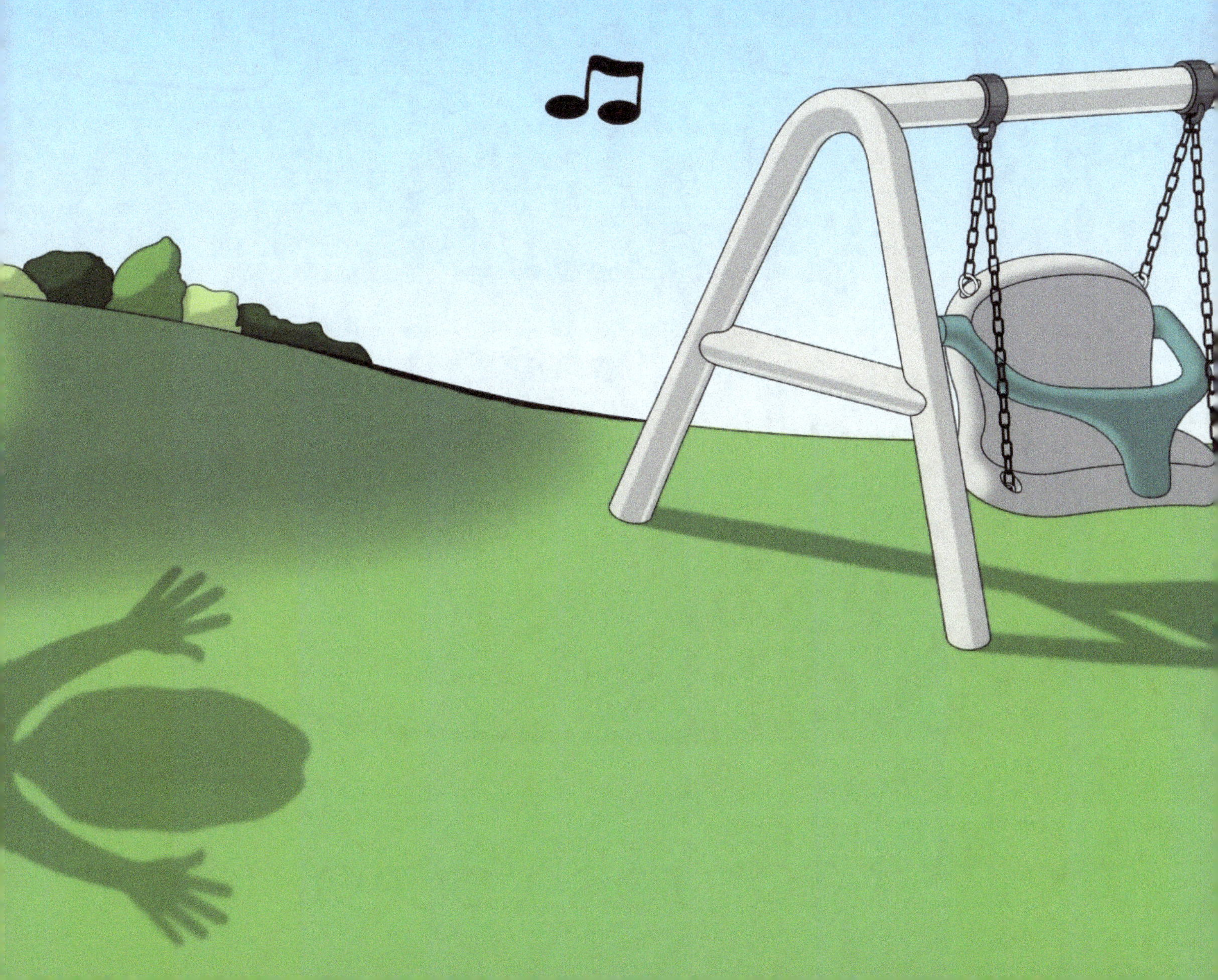

♫ wave our hands, ♪

tap our heads, tap-tap-tap-tap-tap.

Mr. Shadow,
my friend,
play with me.
I'm so happy to
see you today!

Shimmy to the left,
shimmy to the right.

Do the twist,
one more time.

Mr. Shadow,
my friend,
play with me.

I'm so happy
to see you
today!

Wind's blowin' at our backs.
Let's run and run and run!

♪ Mr. Shadow, my friend, play with me. ♫

 I'm so happy to see you today!

I'm happy inside,
see my smile!

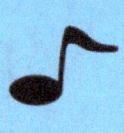

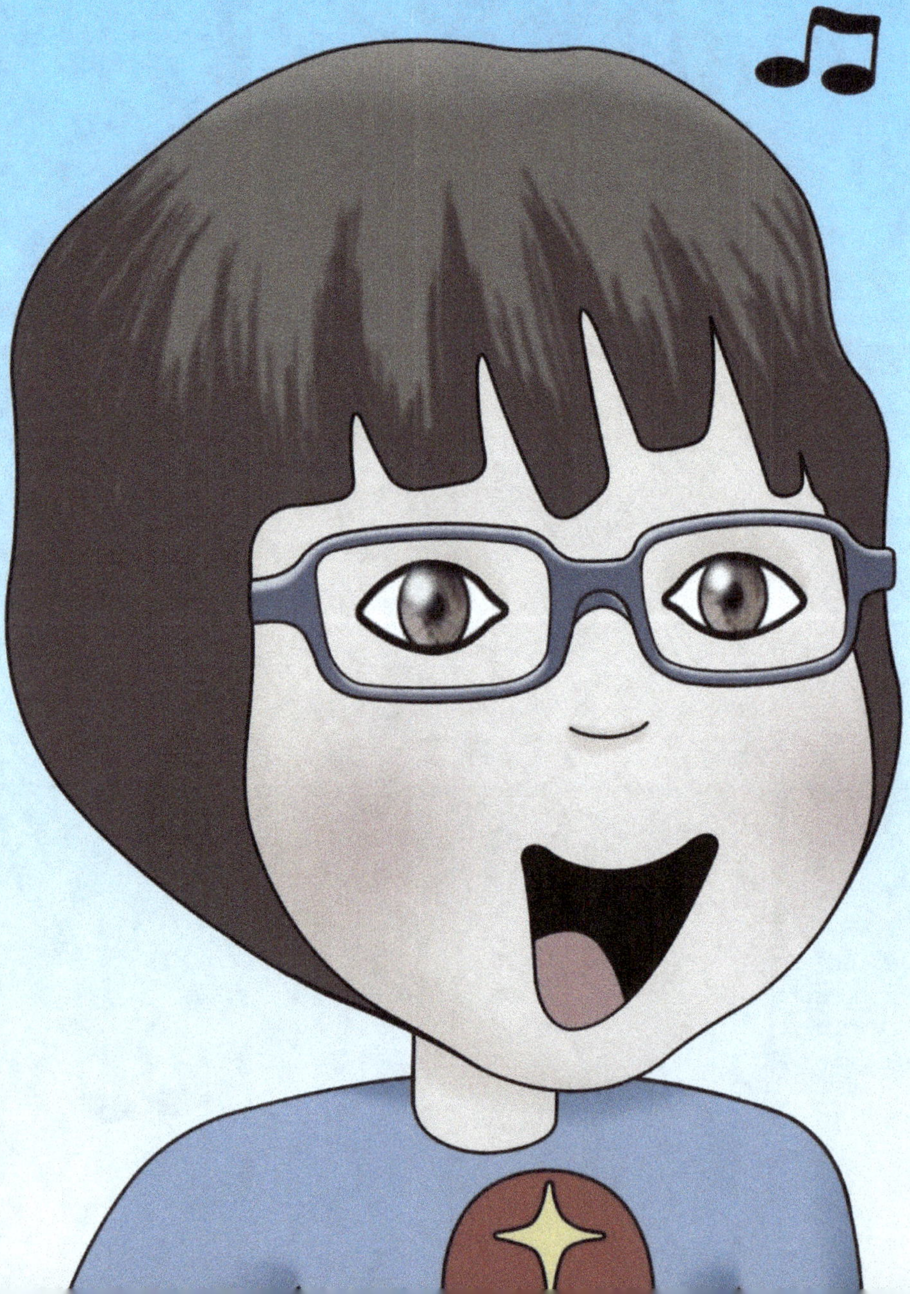

www.ingramcontent.com/pod-product-compliance
Lightning Source LLC
Chambersburg PA
CBHW082104280426
43661CB00089B/846